PRENTICE HALL MATHEMATICS

GRADE 6
GRADE 7
GRADE 8

Test-Taking Strategies
with Transparencies

PEARSON

Prentice
Hall

Boston, Massachusetts
Upper Saddle River, New Jersey

Pearson Prentice Hall™ is a trademark of Pearson Education, Inc.
Pearson® is a registered trademark of Pearson plc.
Prentice Hall® is a registered trademark of Pearson Education, Inc.

ISBN: 0-13-165872-7
5 6 7 8 9 10   10 09 08 07

Test-Taking Strategies With Transparencies

Contents

Practice Masters

Course 1

Course 2

Contents *(continued)*

Course 3

Transparencies

How to Use

These transparencies are designed to familiarize students with common standardized test formats and strategies. The range of strategies includes:

- estimating the answer

- eliminating answers

- answering the question asked

- working backward

- using a variable

- measuring to solve

- drawing a picture

In addition, several common-sense tips are contained in an overview. Most transparencies provide a summary of a test-taking strategy, a worked-out example of the strategy, and two or three exercises for practice.

To make the best use of these transparencies, you will want to spend a few minutes discussing the example. Then, let students work individually on the exercises for a short time before discussing the answers to the exercises. It should take about 10–15 minutes of class time for one transparency.

You can increase the effectiveness of these transparencies in these ways:

- Cover up the exercises while discussing the example. Time the students' work through the exercises. Allow 1–2 minutes per exercise (4–5 minutes per open-ended exercise). This will give students practice allocating their time.

- Present transparencies on days when related mathematical ideas or strategies are presented as part of the regular lessons. This will help students see how these ideas or strategies can be translated into a testing situation.

- Present a transparency right before a test. Then give students one or two test problems that make use of the strategy. This will provide immediate motivation to internalize the ideas presented, and the test questions will reinforce the ideas in a realistic setting.

A student practice master is provided for each chapter's Test-Taking Strategy in Prentice Hall Mathematics *Course 1, Course 2,* and *Course 3.* These practice masters may be used in addition to the practice provided at the end of each chapter in the Student Edition.

Common Features of Standardized Tests

Here, we have displayed common features of several standardized tests.

- Stanford Achievement Test Series, 10th edition (SAT10)

- TerraNova Test

- Iowa Test of Basic Skills (ITBS)

- Iowa Test of Educational Development (ITED)

- Metropolitan Achievement Tests, 8th edition (MAT8)

The information is current as of April 2006. Up-to-date information can be found at each website.

	Choices/Items	Penalty for Guessing	Grid-In Free Responses	Open-Ended Questions	Formulas Given
SAT10	4		No	Yes	No
TerraNova	4		No	Yes	Yes for levels 19, 20, 21, 22
ITBS ITED	5	No	No	No	No
MAT8	4	No	No	No	No

Common Features of Standardized Tests

Calculators	Major Mathematics Sections or Topics	Customization Options	Support Materials Available	Website
Optional on Problem Solving Section	1. Problem Solving 2. Procedures	Can add local items	For Parents For Students For Educators	www.harcourtassessment.com
Optional except for one subtest	Focus is on mathematical reasoning and solving real world problems	Complete Battery Basic Battery Survey Battery	For Educators	www.ctb.com
Optional on Problem Solving and Data Interpretation sections	1. Concepts 2. Estimation 3. Problem Solving 4. Data Interpretation	Complete Battery Survey Battery	For Parents For Students For Educators	www.riverpub.com
Optional on Concepts and Problem Solving subtest	1. Concepts and Problem Solving 2. Procedures	Can be matched to local curriculum and testing requirements	For Parents For Students For Educators	www.harcourtassessment.com

Blank Grids for Gridded Responses

1.

2.

3.

4.

5.

6.

7.

8.

9.

10.

11.

12.

Test-Taking Strategies

Writing Gridded Responses
....

Exercises

Mark your answers on the grid for each exercise.

1. $5.32 + 4$

2. $4.8 \div 0.12$

3. 1.5×20

4. $17.3 - 14.88$

5. $6.5 - (4.1 + 0.6)$

6. You have $440 in a bank. You add $4 per week to the bank for the next six weeks. What is your balance at the end of six weeks?

Answering the Question Asked
••

Exercises

Solve by answering the question asked.

1. A family's monthly expenses are summarized in the circle graph at the right.

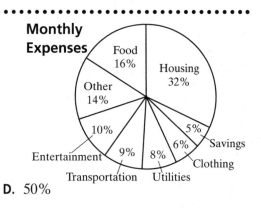

   Monthly Expenses

   a. What percent of their income does the family spend on food *and* housing? Explain.

   A. 16%   **B.** 32%   **C.** 48%   **D.** 50%

   _____

   _____

   _____

   b. What percent of their income does the family save?

   F. 5%   **G.** 6%   **H.** 8%   **J.** 9%

   c. What percent of their income does the family *not* spend on food, clothing or housing?

   A. 16%   **B.** 48%   **C.** 54%   **D.** 46%

2. The table at the right shows the number of boys participating in various sports at a high school.

Sport	Boys Participating
Baseball	21
Basketball	34
Football	62
Track	16
Wrestling	14

   a. How many boys participated in a sport other than football? Explain.

   F. 62   **G.** 21   **H.** 34   **J.** 85

   _____

   _____

   _____

   _____

   b. How many boys participated in basketball *or* football?

   A. 34   **B.** 96   **C.** 62   **D.** 86

Name _____ Class _____ Date _____

Writing Short Responses
Exercises

Use the rubric below to answer each question.

Scoring Rubric
2 The variable is defined, the equation and the method used to solve it are correct, and the correct units are indicated. The solution is correct.
1 The variable is not defined, and there is no equation. However, there is a method to show how the problem was solved and the correct units are indicated.
1 A variable is defined, and an equation is written and solved. The response may contain minor errors.
0 There is no response, it is completely incorrect, or it is the correct response but there is no procedure shown.

1. The price of a skateboard is $74.95 plus tax. The total cost is $79.82. Define a variable. Write and solve an equation to find the amount of tax on the skateboard.

   Three responses are below with the points each received.

2 points	**1 point**	**1 point**
Let t = amount of tax. $74.95 + t = 79.82$ $74.95 + t = 79.82$ $-74.95 \quad -74.95$ $t = 4.87$ The amount of the tax is $4.87.	$79.82 - 74.95 = 4.87$ $4.87	Let t = amount of tax. $74.95 + t = 79.82$ $74.95 + t = 79.82$ $-74.95 \quad -74.95$ $t = 5.87$

   a. Explain why the second response received only 1 point.

   _____

   b. Explain why the third response received only 1 point.

   _____

   c. Write a different equation that could have been used to solve this problem.

   _____

   d. What type of answers might receive zero points?

   _____

2. The price of a model car is $16.45 plus the cost of the glue. The total cost is $17.50. Define a variable. Write and solve an equation to find the cost of the glue. Explain why the following response only received 1 point.
   "Let g = the cost of the glue. $16.45 + g = 17.50; g = 1.25"

   _____

Writing Extended Responses

Exercises

David has one quarter, three dimes, and five nickels. How many different ways can he combine the coins to make 45¢?

Scoring Rubric

- **4 points:** Student correctly answers question in a complete sentence, provides an explanation, and shows all possible combinations..

- **3 points:** Student answers question in a complete sentence, provides an explanation, and shows possible combinations, but makes minor calculation errors.

- **2 point:** Student provides an incorrect explanation and does not completely answer the question.

- **1 point:** Student incorrectly answers the question and does not provide an explanation.

- **0 points:** No response or answer is completely incorrect.

Three responses to the question are shown below.

4 point response	3 point response	1 point response
1 quarter, 2 dimes	1 quarter, 2 dimes	1 quarter, 2 dimes
1 quarter, 1 dime, 2 nickels	1 quarter, 1 dime, 2 nickels	
1 quarter, 4 nickels	1 quarter, 3 nickels	1 quarter, 1 dime, 2 nickels
3 dimes, 3 nickels	3 dimes, 3 nickels	
2 dimes, 5 nickels	2 dimes, 5 nickels	1 quarter, 4 nickels
There are no other possible ways for the coins to add up to 45¢ so this must be the complete answer.	These are the only combinations that add up to 45¢.	2 dimes, 5 nickels

1. Tell why the 4-point response received the points it did.

   _____

   _____

2. Read the 3-point response. What error did the student make?

   _____

3. Write a 2-point response that has an incorrect explanation.

   _____

   _____

Reading for Understanding
Exercises

Use the passage that begins each exercise to answer the parts of the exercise.

1. Mr. Whitby's long-distance phone plan includes a $4.95 per month maintenance fee, $0.10 per minute for long-distance calls made from 6:00 A.M. to 6:00 P.M., and $0.05 per minute for long distance calls made after 6:00 P.M.

   In January, Mr. Whitby only made two long-distance calls. He made one of the calls at noon and the call lasted 17 minutes. He made the other call at 6:30 P.M. He finished this call at 6:53 P.M. How long did Mr. Whitby's second call last?

   a. What is the question asking for?

   _____

   b. Identify the information you need to solve the problem.

   _____

   c. How many minutes did Mr. Whitby's second call last?

   _____

   d. What was the cost of Mr. Whitby's first long-distance call in January?

   _____

   e. What was the cost of Mr. Whitby's second call?

   _____

   f. What was Mr. Whitby's total long-distance bill for January?

   _____

2. Mrs. Wilkinson has two apple trees and one pear tree in her backyard. Each apple tree produced $1\frac{3}{4}$ bushels of apples. The pear tree produced $2\frac{1}{3}$ bushels of pears.

   a. Which produced more per tree, the apple tree or the pear tree? How much more?

   _____

   b. How many total bushels of fruit did Mrs. Wilkinson's trees produce?

   _____

Eliminating Answers

Exercises

Identify the answer choices you can immediately eliminate. Cross the choices out and explain why you eliminated them. Then solve the problem.

1. Sandra is making 4 batches of cookies, so she will need to use 4 times the amount of flour the recipe calls for. The recipe calls for $3\frac{1}{4}$ cups of flour. How much flour does Sandra need?

   A. 12 cups   **B.** $1\frac{1}{4}$ cups   **C.** 13 cups   **D.** 17 cups

2. Alice's grandmother made a quilt that is $9\frac{1}{2}$ feet wide and $12\frac{5}{8}$ feet long. Alice plans to make a quilt that is half as wide and half as long. What will be the dimensions of Alice's quilt?

   F. $4\frac{3}{4}$ ft wide by $6\frac{5}{16}$ ft long   **G.** $4\frac{5}{8}$ ft wide by $6\frac{3}{8}$ ft long

   H. 4 ft wide by 6 ft long   **J.** $18\frac{1}{4}$ ft wide by $24\frac{1}{8}$ ft long

3. There are 95 different kinds of butterflies in a zoo. There are $\frac{4}{5}$ as many different kinds of beetles as butterflies at the zoo. How many different kinds of beetles are at the zoo?

   A. 76 beetles   **B.** 50 beetles   **C.** 120 beetles   **D.** 75 beetles

Working Backward

Exercises

Solve by working backward.

1. 72 is 40% of some number. Find the number.

   A. 28   **B.** 120   **C.** 180   **D.** 240

2. Solve the equation. $4x + 17 = 37$

   F. $x = 3$ **G.** $x = 5$ **H.** $x = 7$ **J.** $x = 10$

3. 75% of what number is 120?

   A. 110   **B.** 125   **C.** 145   **D.** 160

4. Solve the equation. $\frac{1}{2}x - 20 = 30$

   F. $x = 50$ **G.** $x = 100$ **H.** $x = 150$ **J.** $x = 200$

5. Adult tickets at the movie theater cost $7.50. Tickets for children under 12 years old cost $5.25. A group of people went to the movies and they paid a total of $97.50. How many of each type of ticket did the group buy?

   A. 8 adult tickets and 6 children tickets

   B. 6 adult tickets and 8 children tickets

   C. 6 adult tickets and 10 children tickets

   D. 4 adult tickets and 12 children tickets

6. Solve the equation. $4y + 60 = 100$

   F. 10   **G.** 20   **H.** 25   **J.** 40

7. 15% of 25 is what number?

   A. 21.25   **B.** 20   **C.** 15   **D.** 3.75

8. For what value of g is the equation true when $x = 10$?

   $\frac{g}{2}(x + 2) = 24$

   F. 2   **G.** 4   **H.** 6   **J.** 10

9. A flat of tulips costs $11.50. A flat of daffodils cost $15.25. A gardener paid $126 and purchased 6 flats of daffodils and a few flats of tulips. How many flats of tulips did the gardener purchase?

   A. 2 flats   **B.** 3 flats   **C.** 4 flats   **D.** 5 flats

Drawing a Picture

Exercises

Draw a diagram to solve each problem.

1. Point Q is the midpoint of $\overline{PR}$. $\overline{SQ}$ is perpendicular to $\overline{PR}$.
   Name two right angles. Explain.

   _____

   _____

   _____

2. An isosceles triangle is placed on top of a square. The base of the
   square is 6 cm and the base of the triangle is also 6 cm. The height of
   the triangle is 5 cm. What is the total area of the figure? Explain.

   _____

   _____

   _____

   _____

3. Point B is the vertex of angle ABC. The measure of angle ABC is
   64°. Ray BD bisects angle ABC. What is the measure of angle
   ABD?

   _____

4. How many lines of symmetry can be drawn through an
   equilateral triangle?

   _____

5. How many lines of symmetry can be drawn through an isosceles
   triangle?

   _____

6. What are the only two quadrilaterals from which you can form
   4 congruent triangles by drawing the diagonals?

   _____

Name ______________________ Class ______________ Date ______________

Measuring to Solve

Exercises

Use a protractor to answer each question.

1. Cathy's table is shaped like the trapezoid at the right.

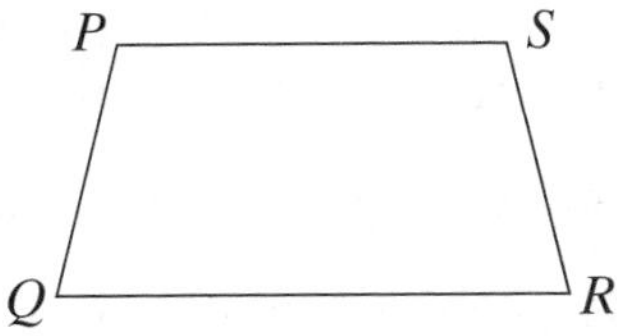

Find the measure of ∠Q to the nearest degree. ______________

2. A quadrilateral is shown at the right.

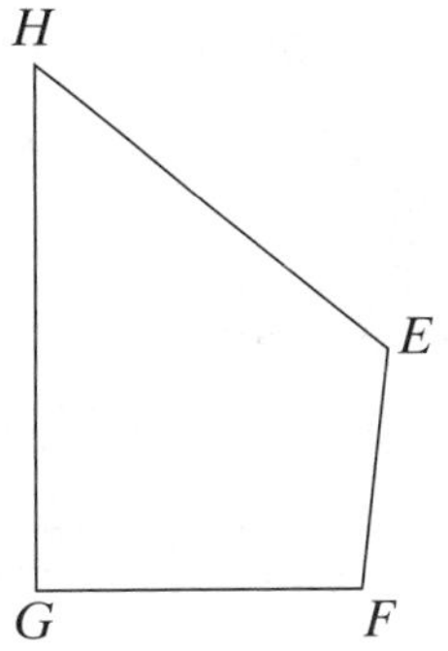

Find the measure of ∠E to the nearest degree. ______________

3. A brace for a shelf is shaped like the triangle at the right.

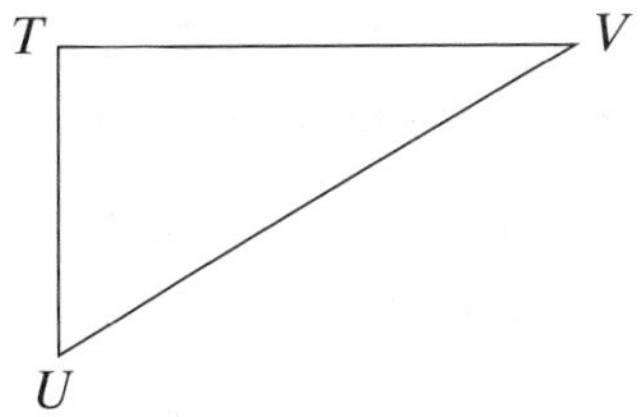

Find the measure of ∠V to the nearest degree. ______________

4. Coulter cuts the shape at the right out of paper.

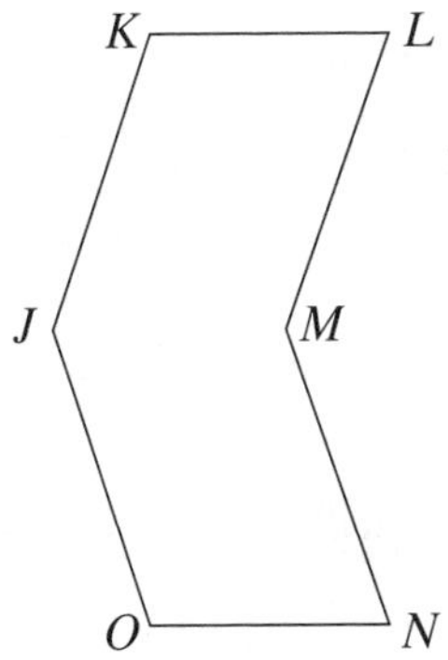

Find the measure of ∠J to the nearest degree. ______________

Name _____ Class _____ Date _____

Interpreting Data
Exercises

Use the graphs at the right to answer each question.

1. Which statement is best supported by the information in the bar graph?

   A. Autumn birthdays were the most common.

   B. Winter birthdays were the least common.

   C. More students in the class were born in Autumn than in Spring.

   D. More students were born in Autumn than in Summer.

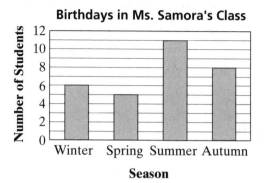

2. Which statement is best supported by the information in the line plot at the right?

   F. Anne received more phone calls on Thursday than she did on Monday.

   G. Anne received fewer than 7 calls on Tuesday.

   H. More than 50% of the calls were received on Friday.

   J. Wednesday was the day on which Anne received the fewest calls.

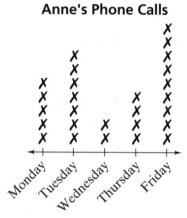

3. What was the mode of the data represented in the line plot?

   A. Monday

   B. Tuesday

   C. Thursday

   D. Friday

4. Which statement is best supported by the information in the bar graph at the right?

   F. George earned more points than Emilio did.

   G. Faye earned the least points.

   H. Two players earned the same number of points.

   J. Hina earned twice as many points as Iko.

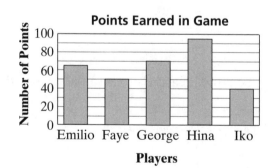

Using a Variable

Exercises

Define a variable. Then write and solve an equation for each problem.

1. Mr. Drake bought 84 horseshoes to shoe all of his horses. Each horse needs 4 shoes. How many horses does Mr. Drake have?

   _____

   _____

2. The price of a DVD is $17.99 plus tax. The total cost is $19.16. How much is the tax on the DVD?

   _____

   _____

3. Ed spends an average of $18 per week on gas. So far, he has spent a total of $216. How many weeks has he bought gas?

   _____

   _____

4. Troop 77 of the Girl Scouts made $342 by selling cookies. If each box of cookies costs $3, how many boxes did Troop 77 sell?

   _____

   _____

5. Maggie spent $30 at the county fair and all she did was go on the rides. If the cost of admission was $8 and each ride cost $2, how many rides did Maggie go on? Let r = the number of rides Maggie went on.

   a. Which equation below could be used to answer the question?

   A. $2r = 30$ **B.** $30 + 2r = 8$

   C. $8 + 2r = 30$ **D.** $8r + 2 = 30$

   b. Solve the equation in part (a) to find the number of rides Maggie rode.

   _____

Estimating the Answer
··
Exercises

Estimate each answer. Use 3 for π. Use estimation to eliminate choices.

1. The diameter of a cylindrical water barrel is 1.8 feet. The height of the barrel is 3.3 feet. Find the volume of the water barrel to the nearest tenth of a cubic foot. Explain your reasoning.

   A. 3.6 ft^3 **B.** 6.4 ft^3 **C.** 8.4 ft^3 **D.** 11.9 ft^3

   _____

   _____

   _____

2. Lisa is having a special dinner and needs to make tablecloths for 10 large round tables. She plans to add 2 feet to the diameter of the tables for the tablecloths, so they will drape over the edges. The diameter of each table is 7.8 feet. Lisa bought 500 square feet of material.

   a. Does she have enough to make all 10 tablecloths? Explain.

   _____

   _____

   _____

   _____

   _____

   _____

   b. If not, approximately how much more material will she need to buy?

   _____

3. The diameter of a round garden is 12 feet. To the nearest square foot, how much plastic would be required to cover the garden?

   F. 36 ft^2 **G.** 48 ft^2 **H.** 72 ft^2 **J.** 108 ft^2

4. To the nearest centimeter, find the circumference of a circle with a 5-centimeter radius.

   A. 15 cm   **B.** 24 cm   **C.** 30 cm   **D.** 75 cm

5. What is the approximate volume of a bucket that has a diameter of 10 inches and is 12 inches tall? _____

Writing Gridded Responses
....

Exercises

**Write what you would grid for each answer. Then grid your answers
on grids provided by your teacher.**

1. Simplify 8(3.6). _____

2. Find the sum of 4.23 and 8.43. _____

3. Find the sum of 12.34 and 45.32. _____

4. Find the difference between 6.8 and -3.4. _____

5. Find $1\frac{1}{2} \div \frac{5}{8}$. _____

6. Solve the proportion. $\frac{4}{12} = \frac{n}{6}$ _____

7. Find the mean of the data set. 3 5 2 9 8 5 3 _____

8. Find the next number in the sequence: $3, -6, 12, -24, \ldots$ _____

9. To get to your grandfather's office, you have to walk up 8 flights of
   stairs each containing 10 steps. How many steps do you walk up?

   _____

10. You have $340 in a bank account. You have decided to add $8
    per week to your account for the next seven weeks. What is your
    balance at the end of four weeks?

    _____

11. A carpenter cuts a 6-m board into 4 equal pieces. What is the
    length in centimeters of each piece?

    _____

12. You spent $14.32 on scrapbook stickers. If each package of
    stickers cost $1.79, how many packages of stickers did you buy?

    _____

13. For your birthday you receive $30. If you buy a CD for $12.99
    and a magazine for $4.95, how much money do you have left?

    _____

14. Software for Mr. Key's new computer costs the following: word
    processing $350, additional graphics $34.99, and tax software
    $79.99. What is the total cost of the software to the nearest dollar?

    _____

15. Margaret can type at a rate of 30 words per minute. At this rate,
    how long would it take her to type 450 words?

    _____

Writing Short Responses

Exercises

Use the scoring rubric below to answer each question.

Scoring Rubric

2 The equation and the solution are correct.

1 There is no equation, but there is a method to show how the answer was achieved.

1 There is an equation and a solution, both of which may contain minor errors. The solution indicates the answer, but does not show units.

0 There is no response, it is completely incorrect, or it is the correct response but there is no procedure shown.

1. During a summer special, costs for bowling at the Swanton Sports Center are $2.75 for shoe rental and $1.50 for each game bowled. Mindy spent $8.75. Write and solve an equation to find how many games she bowled.

   a. Explain why each response above received the indicated points.

2 points	1 point	0 points
Let x = number of games. $2.75 + 1.50x = 8.75$ $1.50x = 6.00$ $\frac{1.50x}{1.50} = \frac{6.00}{1.50}$ $x = 4$ Mindy played 4 games.	$2.75 + 1.50x = 8.75$ $1.50x = 6.00$ $x = 9$ 9 games	3 games

   _____

   _____

   _____

   b. Write a 1-point response that does not have an equation.

   _____

2. While school shopping Marcus spent a total of $63.93. His purchase included a new pair of jeans for $21.99 and some T-shirts for $6.99 each.

   a. Write and solve an equation to find how many T-shirts he bought.

   b. Write a 2-point response.

2 points	1 point	0 points
	$6.99t - 21.99 = 63.93$ $6.99t = 85.92$ $t = 12.29$ 12 T-shirts	7 T-shirts

Reading for Understanding

Exercises

Use the passage to complete Exercises 1–4.

> Cedar Point in Sandusky, Ohio, boasts one of the tallest roller
> coasters in the United States. The Millennium Force measures in
> at 310 feet. After riders reach the top of the first hill, they plunge
> 93 miles per hour down a 300-foot drop at an 80-degree angle.
> For the 2-minute, 20-second ride, riders are seated in one of three
> 36-passenger trains and travel along its 6,595-foot-long track.

1. How tall is the Millennium Force's tallest hill?

    _____

2. How many seconds does each ride take?

    _____

3. The three trains together can complete about 44 rides in an hour.
    How many passengers can ride in one hour?

    _____

4. How many miles long is the track? (Hint: 5,280 feet = 1 mile)

    _____

Use the passage to complete Exercises 5–7.

> The giraffe is one of the heaviest land animals. Large males can weigh
> up to 1,900 kg. Females are smaller and rarely reach half the weight of
> the males. A giraffe's neck and long legs combine to make the giraffe
> one of the tallest of all animals, averaging about 17 feet tall for a male.
> The giraffe's neck, supported by seven elongated vertebrae, can
> measure even longer than its 1.8-m (6-ft) legs. A giraffe's long legs
> give it the ability to run at a top speed of about 56 km/h (35 mi/h).

5. What is the weight of a large giraffe in pounds? (Hint: There are
    2.2 pounds per kilogram.)

    _____

6. What is the weight of a female giraffe, in kilograms?

    _____

7. How far could a giraffe travel at its top speed in fifteen minutes?

    _____

Writing Extended Responses
....
Exercises

Use the scoring rubric shown to answer each question.

Scoring Rubric
4 Identifies the variables, shows all work, and answers all parts of the problem.
3 Identifies the variable, shows work, and answers all parts of the problem. There may be a computational error.
1 Problem set up incorrectly, does not answer all parts of the problem and contains errors.

1. Parts to fix your truck cost you $115.95. The mechanic charges $42 per hour for labor. The final bill you receive is $241.95. How long did the mechanic work on your truck? Write and solve an equation. Show all your work.

4 points	3 points
Let h = hours worked.	Let h = hours worked.
$42h + 115.95 = 241.95$	$42h + 115.95 = 241.95$
$42h + 115.95 - 115.95 = 241.95 - 115.95$	$42h = 357.90$
$42h = 126$	$\frac{42h}{42} = \frac{357.90}{42}$
$\frac{42h}{42} = \frac{126}{42}$	$h = 8.5$
$h = 3$	8.5 hours
The mechanic worked a total of 3 hours on the truck.	

  a. Read the 3-point response. What error was made?

  _____

  _____

  b. Write what you think a 2-point response to the problem would look like.

  _____

2. Aaron works at Hobby Town and has 256 purple bracelet beads and 96 orange bracelet beads to repackage. Each new bag must contain the same number of purple beads and the same number of orange beads. Aaron wants to make as many bags as possible. How many bags can he make? How many beads of each color will Aaron put in each new bag?

  a. Write a 4-point response to the problem.

  _____

  _____

  _____

  b. Write a 1-point response to the problem.

  _____

Using a Variable

Exercises

Use a variable to write an equation and solve each problem.

1. A lunch platter contains a variety of luncheon meats. To serve 12 people, $3\frac{1}{2}$ pounds of meat are needed. How many pounds of meat are needed to serve 18 people?

   _____

2. If 80 kg of cement are used to make 400 kg of concrete, how much cement is needed to make 1,600 kg of concrete?

   _____

3. A machine produces 2,070 flashlights in 8.5 hours. How many flashlights will the machine produce in 40 hours?

   _____

4. You receive $72.96 for working an 8-hour day. How much would you receive for working a 32-hour week?

   _____

5. A clothing manufacturer is shipping sweaters to a department store. The manufacturer has previously shipped 330 sweaters in 18 boxes. At this rate, how many boxes would the manufacturer need to ship 550 sweaters?

   _____

6. The monthly payment on a loan is $29.50 for every $1,000 borrowed. At this rate, find the monthly payment for a $9,000 car loan.

   _____

7. Nine ceramic tiles are required to cover four square feet. At this rate, how many square feet can be tiled with 270 ceramic tiles?

   _____

8. A quality control inspector found three defective computer chips in a shipment of 500 chips. At this rate, how many computer chips would be defective in a shipment of 3,000 chips?

   _____

9. The ratio of chicory to coffee in a New England coffee mixture is $1 : 8$. If the coffee company uses 85 pounds of chicory for a batch of coffee mixture, how many pounds of coffee are needed?

   _____

10. In preparing a banquet for 30 people, a restaurant cook uses nine pounds of potatoes. How many pounds of potatoes will be needed for a banquet for 175 people?

    _____

Working Backward

•••

Exercises

Solve each problem by working backward. Circle the correct answer.

1. Your grades on five math tests are 95, 86, 79, 88, and 93. What grade do you need on the sixth test to have an average of 90?

   A. 76   **B.** 90   **C.** 99   **D.** 100

2. The surface area of a cube is 294 square feet. What is the length (in feet) of each edge of the cube? [Hint: $S = 6s^2$]

   F. -7 feet   **G.** 7 feet   **H.** 49 feet   **J.** 64 feet

3. If $7x - 17 = 32$, what is the value of x?

   A. 2.14   **B.** 5   **C.** 7   **D.** 9

4. What is the greatest number of theater tickets you can buy if you have $227.18 and each theater ticket costs $42.75?

   F. 4 tickets   **G.** 5 tickets   **H.** 6 tickets   **J.** 7 tickets

5. If you start with a number, multiply by 3, then subtract 16, the result is 152. What is the number?

   A. 37   **B.** 48   **C.** 51   **D.** 56

6. A CD player is on sale for $54.99. The CD player has been discounted 25%. What is the original price of the CD player?

   F. $13.75   **G.** $68.74   **H.** $73.32   **J.** $75.00

7. If $\frac{3}{8} = \frac{x}{32}$, then $x = $ _____ .

   A. 4   **B.** 12   **C.** 24   **D.** 96

8. The formula for the area of a triangle is $A = \frac{1}{2}bh$. If the area of a triangle is 48 square feet and the height is 6 feet, what is the length of the base?

   F. 12 feet   **G.** 16 feet   **H.** 24 feet   **J.** 48 feet

9. Juan can buy one ice cream cone for $.90. What is the greatest number of ice cream cones he can buy for $6.00?

   A. 3 cones   **B.** 4 cones   **C.** 5 cones   **D.** 6 cones

10. A train left New York at 1:20 A.M. and reached its stop $3\frac{1}{4}$ hours later. What time did the train reach its stop?

    F. 4:35 A.M.   **G.** 4:45 A.M.   **H.** 5:20 A.M.   **J.** 6:00 A.M.

11. If $\frac{x}{8} = 114$, what is the value of x?

    A. 14.25   **B.** 112   **C.** 812   **D.** 912

Drawing a Picture
Exercises

Draw a diagram to solve each exercise.

1. $\triangle ABC \cong \triangle DEF$. The measure of $\angle A = 51°$, and the measure of $\angle C = 94°$. What is the measure of $\angle E$?

   _____

2. On a bus line, three towns are represented by points G, H, and J. Town G is 55 miles north of Town H, and Town J is 10 mi south of Town G. Which town is between the other two?

   _____

3. The angle bisector of one angle of a triangle measures 42°. The angle bisector of another angle of the triangle measures 36°. What is the measure of the third angle of the triangle?

   _____

4. Team L and Team M have a tug of war. From their starting positions Team L pulls Team M forward 3 meters, and Team L is then pulled forward 5 meters. Team M then pulls Team L forward 4 meters. If the first team to be pulled forward 10 meters loses, how many more meters must Team M pull Team L forward to win?

   _____

5. On a number line point A is 5 units to the left of point B. Point A is located at coordinate -7.2. What is the coordinate of point B?

   _____

6. Circle M has a diameter of 12 inches. Radii $\overline{MN}$ and $\overline{MP}$ form an angle that is not a straight angle. The length of $\overline{NP}$ is *not* 12 inches. Classify $\triangle MNP$ according to its sides.

   _____

7. During a sightseeing tour in Washington D.C., the tour bus travels 4 blocks due north, 6 blocks due east, 12 blocks due south, 22 blocks due west, and 8 blocks due north. At this point, where is the tour bus in relation to its starting point?

   _____

8. How many diagonals can be drawn in a hexagon?

   _____

9. Rectangle $ABCD$ has a perimeter of 62. If the length of $\overline{AD}$ is 14, what is the area of $ABCD$?

   _____

Measuring to Solve

Exercises

Use a ruler to answer each question.

1. The bottom of a soup can is circular, as shown at the right. Measure the radius of the circle in centimeters. Find the circumference of the circle. Use 3.14 for π.

_____

2. The front of a box of cereal is a rectangle, as shown at the right. Measure the dimensions of the rectangle in centimeters. Find the perimeter of the rectangle.

_____

3. A box of tea bags is a cube. The top of the box is the square shown at the right. Measure the dimensions of the square. Find the area of the square.

_____

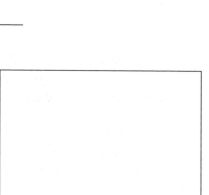

Name _____ Class _____ Date _____

Estimating the Answer
Exercises

Estimate each answer. Circle the letter of the best answer.

1. The circumference of a circle is about 24 ft. Which is closest to the length of the diameter of the circle?

   A. 8 ft   **B.** 9 ft   **C.** 10 ft   **D.** 11 ft

2. Farmer's Merchantile is offering a 30% discount on all farm gates. Which is closest to the discount price of a farm gate that regularly costs $130?

   F. $40   **G.** $90   **H.** $100   **J.** $120

3. The lengths of two legs of a right triangle are 5 ft and 10 ft. Which is closest to the length of the hypotenuse?

   A. 10 ft   **B.** 11 ft   **C.** 13 ft   **D.** 15.5 ft

4. Which is the best estimate for the mean of the data set?
   30, 34, 25, 30, 38, 32

   F. 40   **G.** 35   **H.** 30   **J.** 25

5. You borrow $500 at a 4% simple interest rate. About how much interest will you owe in 2 years?

   A. $20   **B.** $40   **C.** $80   **D.** $520

6. On Friday, $\frac{5}{9}$ of the students at school bought pizza for lunch. About what percent of the students did *not* buy pizza for lunch?

   F. 35%   **G.** 45%   **H.** 55%   **J.** 65%

7. Four pieces of trim, each $8\frac{1}{2}$-inches long are cut from a board 100 inches long. About how many inches of board remain?

   A. 34 inches   **B.** 50 inches   **C.** 66 inches   **D.** 75 inches

8. Linden bought a jacket for 15% off the regular retail price of $110. What did Linden pay for the jacket?

   F. $16.50   **G.** $65.60   **H.** $75.80   **J.** $93.50

Name _____ Class _____ Date _____

Answering the Question Asked
Exercises

Use the table below to answer exercises 1–4.

Record Breakers

What	Name	Size
Deepest Lake	Baikal	5,315 feet deep
Largest Continent	Asia	17,212,041 square miles
Lowest Land Point	Dead Sea	1,349 feet below sea level
Largest Gorge	Grand Canyon	277 miles long, up to 18 miles wide, 1 mile deep
Longest Mountain Range	Andes	more than 5,000 miles
Longest River	Nile	4,145 miles
Shortest River	Roe	201 feet

1. What is the longest river?

   A. Nile   **B.** Roe   **C.** Andes   **D.** Baikal

2. What is the difference between the longest and shortest river, in feet?

   F. 3,944 feet   **G.** 4,346 feet   **H.** 2,189 feet   **J.** 2.189×10^7 feet

3. At its widest point, what is the volume of the Grand Canyon?

   A. 4,986 miles^3 **B.** 3,256 miles^3 **C.** 296 miles^3 **D.** 295 miles^3

4. What is the difference in length between the longest mountain range and the longest river?

   F. 300 miles   **G.** 855 miles   **H.** 1,000 miles   **J.** 2,290 miles

Use the double bar graph for exercises 5–7.

5. Which of the following continents had the least amount of change in wheat production per 1,000 capita between 1961 and 2000?

   A. Africa   **B.** Asia

   C. North America   **D.** South America

6. What is the approximate change in Europe's wheat production per 1,000 capita from 1961 to 2000?

   F. 100 tons   **G.** 150 tons

   H. 170 tons   **J.** 200 tons

7. In 2000, what is the approximate mean of wheat produced for all continents shown?

   A. 200 tons   **B.** 250 tons

   C. 300 tons   **D.** 350 tons

Wheat Production per 1,000 Capita by Continent

Name _____ Class _____ Date _____

Interpreting Data
Exercises

Use the graphs at the right to answer each question.

1. What is the median of the scores shown in the stem-and-leaf plot at the right?

   A. 6   **B.** 8   **C.** 81   **D.** 86

Scores on Science Test

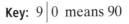

9	0 0 1 3 5 7 7 8
8	0 1 1 1 2 3 6 8 8 9
7	6 8 8 9
6	7

Key: 9 | 0 means 90

2. What is the range of the scores shown in the stem-and-leaf plot at the right?

   F. 9   **G.** 23   **H.** 31   **J.** 86

3. Which statement is best supported by the information in the bar graph at the right?

   A. More girls voted for "Pandas" than voted for "Tigers."

   B. The total number of votes for "Pandas" was the same as the total number of votes for "Dragons."

   C. The same number of girls voted for "Dragons" as voted for "Tigers."

   D. The fewest number of votes went to "Tigers."

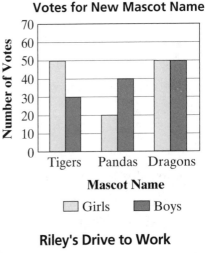

4. Which statement is NOT supported by the information in the line graph at the right?

   F. It took Riley approximately 40 minutes to drive to work.

   G. Riley's maximum speed on the way to work is about 58 miles per hour.

   H. Riley stops 4 times on his way to work.

   J. Riley's maximum speed for the first 10 minutes of the drive is about 20 miles per hour.

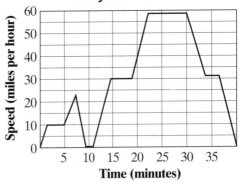

Eliminating Answers
Exercises

Solve each problem.

1. A quality-control inspector found 40 defective crayons out of 1,000 that she checked. What percent of the crayons were defective?

   A. 400%   **B.** 100%   **C.** 40%   **D.** 4%

   a. Explain why you can eliminate answer choices A and C.

   _____

   b. What is the correct answer choice? _____

2. A bag contains 6 green apples, 8 red apples, and 16 yellow apples. What is the probability that an apple selected at random is yellow?

   F. $\frac{1}{8}$ **G.** $\frac{4}{15}$ **H.** $\frac{8}{15}$ **J.** 1

   a. Explain why you can eliminate answer choices F and J.

   _____

   _____

   b. What is the correct answer choice? _____

3. At a carnival you have the chance to spin the letter wheel. The letter wheel has 26 spaces, each with a different letter of the alphabet. You spin the spinner twice. Find $P(C, \text{then } H)$.

   A. $\frac{1}{2}$ **B.** $\frac{1}{26}$ **C.** $\frac{1}{52}$ **D.** $\frac{1}{676}$

   a. Explain why you can eliminate answer choices A and B.

   _____

   _____

   b. What is the correct answer choice? _____

4. How many three-number permutations can be formed from the numbers 1, 2, 3, 4, and 5, if no digit is used more than once?

   F. 240   **G.** 120   **H.** 60   **J.** 30

   a. Explain why you can eliminate answer choices F and G.

   _____

   _____

   b. What is the correct answer choice? _____

Writing Gridded Responses
Exercises

Mark your answers on the grid for each exercise.

1. Amanda is 14 cm taller than her sister, Rachel. The sum of their heights is 96 cm. How many centimeters tall is Amanda?

2. The record high temperature for January in Cleveland, OH was 73°F in 1950. The record low temperature for January, −20°F, occurred in 1994. What is the difference (in degrees) between these temperatures?

3. Evaluate $|7 - 5h|$ for $h = 9$.

4. Peaches were on sale for $1.49 per pound. Zoe bought three pounds and gave the cashier a $10 bill. How much change, in dollars, does Zoe receive?

5. Simplify. $\dfrac{-128}{-4}$

6. The area of a rectangle is 72 cm^2. The length is 6 cm greater than the width. How many centimeters long is the rectangle?

Writing Short Responses
Exercises

Use the scoring rubric shown to answer each question.

Scoring Rubric

2 The equation and solution are correct.

1 There is no equation, but there is a method to show the correct solution.

1 There is an equation and a solution but they contain minor errors.

0 There is no response, or the solution is completely incorrect.

A carpet cleaning service charges a flat fee of $50 plus $15 per room to clean the carpet in a home. A family paid $185 to have their carpet cleaned. Write and solve an equation to find out how many rooms they have.

2 points	1 point	0 points
Let x = the number of rooms. $$50 + 15x = 185$$ $$15x = 135$$ $$\frac{15x}{15} = \frac{135}{15}$$ $$x = 9$$ The family has 9 rooms.	$185 - 50 = 135$ $\frac{135}{15} = 9$ 9	$50x + 15 = 185$ $65x = 185$ $x = 2.85$ 3 rooms

1. Explain why each response above received the indicated points.

   _____

   _____

   _____

   _____

   _____

   _____

2. Write a two-point response for the following problem: Doreen bought three identical ceramic figurines and paid a flat fee of $12.50 to have them glazed. If her bill (before taxes) came to $39.47, how much was each figurine?

   _____

   _____

Writing Extended Responses

Exercises

Use the scoring rubric shown to solve the problem.

To receive full credit, you must: (1) define variables and write two correct linear equations, (2) graph each equation with the correct slope and *y*-intercept, and (3) find the break-even point. The number of points for different types of answers is as follows.

Scoring Rubric

4 The equations, the graphs, and the solution are correct.

3 The equations and the graphs are correct, but the solution is incorrect.

2 There are equations, graphs, and a solution, some of which have minor errors in them.

1 The variables are chosen and defined. The equations, the graphs, and the solution have many flaws in them.

0 There is no response, the answer is completely incorrect, or it is a correct response but no procedure is shown.

The Student Council at North High School is selling picture frames for Spirit Day. The frames cost $1.50 each and a flat fee of $10.50 for shipping. The Student Council plans to sell the frames for $2.25 each. Write the equations for expenses and income. Solve the system by graphing to find how many picture frames they must sell to break even.

1. Write a 4-point solution to this problem.

_____

_____

_____

2. How many points should a student receive for the solution shown at the right? Explain.

$10.50 \div 0.75 = 14$
The answer is 14.

_____

_____

Using a Variable
Exercises

Define a variable. Then, write and solve an equation for each problem.

1. In a bag, the ratio of red marbles to blue marbles is 9 to 21. The bag contains 30 red marbles. How many blue marbles are in the bag?

   _____

2. The Sampson family is building a playhouse. The scale of their blueprint is 2.5 cm : 12 ft. The playhouse will be 24 ft wide and 30 ft long. Find the dimensions on the blueprint.

   _____

   _____

3. A 3 ft high fire hydrant casts a 5 ft long shadow. Gena is standing nearby and casts an 8.5 ft long shadow. How tall is Gena?

   _____

4. A family is on a 520-mi road trip. They have driven 195 mi in 3 hours. If they continue driving at this rate, how long will it take them to drive the entire 520 mi?

   _____

5. An architect's drawing of a museum is 18 cm wide by 28 cm long. The actual building is going to be 45 m wide. How long will the building be?

   _____

6. A painter is mixing paint. The directions say to mix red, blue, and yellow paint in a ratio of 3 : 7 : 6. He needs a gallon of paint. How many ounces of each color does the painter need?

   _____

   _____

   _____

7. A seamstress can make two dresses in nine hours.

   a. At this rate, how long will it take her to make seven dresses?

   _____

   b. How many dresses can she make in 15 hours?

   _____

Estimating the Answer

Exercises

Estimate each answer.

1. Ted collects rare gold coins. He bought one coin in his collection for $32.85. Five years later, the coin was worth $54.79. Use estimating to find the percent of increase in the value of the coin.

   A. 21.94%　　　　**B.** 40%　　　　**C.** 50%　　　　**D.** $66\frac{2}{3}$ %

2. Georgianne wants to leave a 20% tip for her $45 haircut. Estimate how much she should tip her hairdresser.

   F. $54　　　　**G.** $9　　　　**H.** $7　　　　**J.** $5

3. In a recent school election, 76% of the students voted for the winning candidate for student council treasurer. If 392 students voted, how many voted for the winning candidate?

   A. 325　　　　**B.** 300　　　　**C.** 275　　　　**D.** 250

4. Estimate 28% of 621.

   F. 280　　　　**G.** 200　　　　**H.** 195　　　　**J.** 180

5. A basketball player made 88% of 48 free-throw attempts in one season. About how many free-throws did the player successfully make during the season?

   A. 45　　　　**B.** 35　　　　**C.** 32　　　　**D.** 9

6. Estimate the selling price of a video game if the percent of markup is 24% and the store's cost is $38.99.

   F. $40　　　　**G.** $50　　　　**H.** $60　　　　**J.** $40

7. Which percent is closest to $\frac{78}{321}$?

   A. 78%　　　　**B.** 40%　　　　**C.** 25%　　　　**D.** $33\frac{1}{3}$ %

8. Jiroko deposits $3,046 into a savings account that earns 6.85% simple interest. Approximately how much money will be in the account at the end of 3 years?

   F. $6,320　　　　**G.** $3,640　　　　**H.** $3,230　　　　**J.** $3,000

9. On the first day of a new release, a video store rented out 72% of its 89 copies of the movie. Approximately how many copies did the video store rent?

   A. 45　　　　**B.** 57　　　　**C.** 63　　　　**D.** 72

10. Estimate the final cost of a CD that costs $12.99 if the tax rate is 5.25%

    F. $13.65　　　　**G.** $14.00　　　　**H.** $15.00　　　　**I.** $15.45

Reading for Understanding

Exercises

Use the passage for the following exercises.

> Since the earliest centuries, artists, musicians, architects, and mathematicians have been intrigued by a figure known as "The Golden Rectangle." The rectangle's pleasant shape has made it popular. A rectangle is a Golden Rectangle if the ratio of its larger side to its smaller side is 1.618 to 1.
>
> Famous artists, including Piet Mondrian, Seurat, and Leonardo Da Vinci, used the Golden Rectangle in their paintings. In music, the Mozart sonatas and Beethoven's Fifth Symphony have been linked to the Golden Rectangle. On the famed Stradivarius violins, placement of the sound holes is also related to the Golden Rectangle.
>
> Most experts agree that the ancient Greek civilization used the Golden Rectangle when building the Parthenon, among other buildings. Finally, the ratio of the base and the height of the ancient Egyptian pyramids is also close to the ratio of the Golden Rectangle.

1. The shorter side of a window is 36 in. The window is shaped like a Golden Rectangle. Find the length of the longer side of the window. Round your answer to the nearest hundredth.

    _____

2. The longer edge of a picture frame is 18 in. The picture frame is shaped like a Golden Rectangle. What is the length of the shorter edge of the picture frame? Round your answer to the nearest hundredth.

    _____

3. The dimensions of a computer screen are 28 cm by 21 cm. Is the shape of the computer screen a Golden Rectangle? Explain.

    _____

    _____

    _____

    _____

Drawing a Picture ··
Exercises

Draw a picture to help you solve each problem.

1. In Nathan's neighborhood, the library (L), the school (S), and the grocery store (G) lie on a straight road in that order. The distance from S to G is 5 times the distance from L to S. The distance from L to G is 28 more than 4 times the distance from L to S. What is the distance between the library and the school?

   _____

2. $R(3, 4)$, $S(8, 4)$, and $T(1, 1)$ are three vertices of two parallelograms, in no particular order. Find the coordinates of U, the fourth vertex in each parallelogram.

   _____

   _____

3. Quadrilateral $JKLM$ has vertices $J(1, 7)$, $K(6, 0)$, $L(1, -7)$ and $M(-4, 0)$. What is the best name for the quadrilateral?

   _____

4. The sides of a parallelogram and one of its diagonals form two isosceles triangles. Must the parallelogram be a rhombus?

   _____

5. Maple Street is parallel to Elm Street. Oak Street is perpendicular to Maple Street. Chestnut Street is perpendicular to Elm Street. Are Chestnut Street and Oak Street parallel?

   _____

6. The light from a night watchman's tower extends 440 yd in all directions. What is the area covered by the night watchman's light? Use 3.14 for π and round to the nearest square yard.

   _____

7. Natalie rides her bike from her house to her friend Jon's house. She rides 5 blocks north, 2 blocks east, 3 blocks north, then 4 blocks east. A path goes straight from her house to Jon's house. How many blocks would she have walked if she had taken the path?

   _____

8. The length of a rectangle is 9 more than 4 times the width. The perimeter of the rectangle is 128 cm. Find the length and width.

   _____

Eliminating Answers

Exercises

Use the following multiple choice question to answer Exercises 1–2.

What is the volume of a square pyramid with a base edge length of 9 ft and a height of 17 ft?

    A. 1,377 ft   **B.** 459 ft^2 **C.** 306 ft^3 **D.** 459 ft^3

1. Which answer choices can be eliminated? Why?

    _____

    _____

    _____

2. Find the correct answer choice. _____

Solve each multiple choice question by eliminating answers.

3. The volume of a cube is 24 m^3. The lengths of the sides are increased by a scale factor of $\frac{6}{5}$. What is the volume of the new cube?

    F. 41.472 m^3 **G.** 192 m^3 **H.** 28.8 m^3 **J.** 34.56 m^3

4. What is the surface area of a cylinder with a radius of 5 cm and a height of 14 m?

    A. 710π m^3 **B.** 190π m^3 **C.** 190π m^2 **D.** 190 m^2

5. A box measuring 5-in.-by-2-in.-by-7 in. is packed inside a gift box that is an 8-in. cube. How much space is left inside for packing materials?

    F. 512 in.^{3} **G.** 442 in.^{3} **H.** 118 in.^{3} **J.** 70 in.^{3}

6. A round table has a diameter of 3 ft. What size tablecloth is needed to have one foot of overhang all around the table?

    A. 19.625 ft^2 **B.** 7.065 ft^2 **C.** 15.7 ft^2 **D.** 12.56 ft^2

7. The surface area of a rectangular prism is 126 in.^{2} The surface area of a similar rectangular prism is 224 in.^{2} What is the ratio of corresponding dimensions of the small prism to the large prism?

    F. $\frac{16}{9}$ **G.** $\frac{4}{3}$ **H.** $\frac{9}{16}$ **J.** $\frac{3}{4}$

Measuring to Solve

Exercises

Use a ruler to answer each question. Round to the nearest tenth, if necessary.

1. The net at the right forms a square prism. Measure its dimensions in centimeters.

   Find the surface area of the prism.

   _____

2. The net at the right forms a triangular pyramid. Measure its dimensions in centimeters.

   Find the surface area of the triangular pyramid.

   _____

3. The net at the right forms a cylinder. Measure its dimensions in centimeters. Use 3.14 for π.
   Find the surface area of the cylinder.

   _____

Answering the Question Asked

Exercises

Read each question carefully. Then solve.

1. James is choosing 4 books from his shelf to take on vacation. His shelf contains 9 books. How many different ways can James choose the books?

   A. 3,024   **B.** 126   **C.** 120   **D.** 36

2. A spinner numbered from one to eight is divided into eight equal sections. What is the probability of spinning a one or an eight?

   F. $\frac{1}{16}$ **G.** $\frac{1}{64}$ **H.** 12.5%   **J.** 25%

3. A bag contains 7 green marbles, 11 red marbles, and 2 blue marbles. What is the probability of *not* drawing a red marble?

   A. 45%   **B.** 40%   **C.** 35%   **D.** 10%

4. A basket of fruit contains 4 apples, 6 oranges, and 5 plums. Deanna chooses 2 pieces of fruit without replacing her first choice. What is the probability she will first choose an orange, then a plum?

   F. $\frac{2}{5}$ **G.** $\frac{1}{3}$ **H.** $\frac{1}{7}$ **J.** $\frac{2}{15}$

5. You deposit $1,500 into an account that pays 4.5% interest compounded annually. How much is in the account at the end of 4 years?

   A. $1,788.78   **B.** $1,770.00   **C.** $1,567.50   **D.** $270.00

6. A jewelry store sells watches, rings, and necklaces. Over time, the jeweler has found that 40% of her customers buy watches and 25% buy necklaces. What is the probability that a person will buy either a watch or a necklace?

   F. 0.65   **G.** 0.40   **H.** 0.35   **J.** 0.25

7. Each letter in the word GEOMETRY appears on a card. You choose a card at random and then replace it. Then you choose a second card. What is the probability that you will draw 2 E's?

   A. $\frac{1}{16}$ **B.** $\frac{2}{15}$ **C.** $\frac{1}{8}$ **D.** $\frac{1}{4}$

8. Fourteen schools compete in a band competition. Gold, silver, and bronze medals are awarded for first, second, and third place. How many different arrangements of winners can there be?

   F. 2,744   **H.** 2,184   **G.** 364   **J.** 39

Interpreting Data

Exercises

Use the graphs at the right to answer each question.

1. The graph shows the percent of time Colin spends practicing each sport. If he has 2 hours to spend practicing, how many minutes will he spend practicing soccer?

   A. 18   **B.** 24
   C. 40   **D.** 48

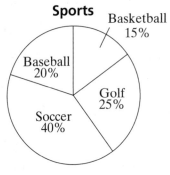

Sports

2. If Colin has 3.5 hours to spend practicing, how many minutes will he spend practicing baseball?

   F. 42   **G.** 84
   H. 40   **J.** 20

3. Predict the weight for a person who is 55 inches tall.

   A. 45 pounds

   B. 55 pounds

   C. 90 pounds

   D. 120 pounds

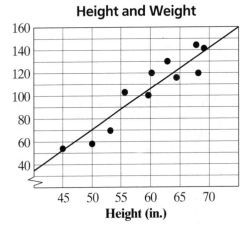

Height and Weight

4. Which statement is NOT supported by the information in the line graph at the right?

   F. As height increases, so does weight.

   G. This graph has a positive trend.

   H. People lose weight as they grow taller.

   J. As a person grows taller, they weigh more.

5. What is the mode of the scores shown in the stem-and-leaf plot at the right?

   A. 4   **B.** 77
   C. 84   **D.** 102

6. What is the range of the scores shown in the stem-and-leaf plot at the right?

   F. 1   **G.** 23
   H. 31   **J.** 84

Golf Scores

7	1 1 2 3 5 7 7 8
8	2 2 3 4 4 4 5 6 8 8 9
9	1 3 4 5 5
10	1 1 2

Key: 7 | 1 means 71

Working Backward

··

Exercises

Solve each of the following by working backward.

1. Solve for x. $5x + 4 = 29$

   A. $x = 2$ **B.** $x = 5$ **C.** $x = 7$ **D.** $x = 12$

2. Consider the function $f(x) = 3x - 7$. What value of x will make $f(x) = 20$?

   F. 53   **G.** 9   **H.** -36 **J.** -80

3. The area of a circle is 15.9 mm^2. What is the diameter of the circle?

   A. 4.5 mm   **B.** 3.14 mm   **C.** 2.25 mm   **D.** 1.05 mm

4. The base of a rectangular prism has a length of 9 in. and a width of 7 in. The volume of the prism is 787.5 in.^{3}. What is the height of the prism?

   F. 87.5 in.   **G.** 63 in.   **H.** 12.5 in.   **J.** 7.875 in.

5. If $x^3 = 64$, find the value of $\frac{x^5}{x^3}$.

   A. 1,024   **B.** 16   **C.** 8   **D.** 4

6. Which number could *not* be a value of y if $y = 5x^2 - 9$?

   F. 11   **G.** -4 **H.** -9 **J.** -10

7. The side lengths of which of the following triangles do *not* form a right triangle?

   A. 12 cm, 16 cm, 20 cm   **B.** 10 cm, 24 cm, 26 cm

   C. 8 cm, 10 cm, 12 cm   **D.** 15 cm, 20 cm, 25 cm

8. Jennie's average after four math tests is an 85. What must Jennie score on the fifth test to raise her grade to an 87?

   F. 100   **G.** 95   **H.** 91   **J.** 87

9. Which ordered pair lies on the line $y = 11x - 13$?

   A. $(2, 9)$ **B.** $(-13, 0)$ **C.** $(0, 11)$ **D.** $(1, 2)$

10. You start an exercise program. You begin by walking 1.5 mi the first day and increase your distance by 0.25 mi per day. How many miles do you walk on the 7th day?

    F. 1.75 mi   **G.** 3 mi   **H.** 3.25 mi   **J.** 3.5 mi

Test-Taking Strategies Course 1 Answers

Writing Gridded Responses

1. 9.32   **2.** 40   **3.** 30
4. 2.42   **5.** 1.8   **6.** 464

Answering the Question Asked

1a. C; The question asks for the percent spent on food *and* housing. Add the two percents for these categories. The total is 16% + 32% = 48%, so the correct answer is choice C.
1b. F
1c. D
2a. J; The question asks for the number of boys who participated in a sport other than football. Add the number of boys who participated in all the other sports. The total is 21 + 34 + 16 + 14 = 85 boys, so the correct answer choice is J.
2b. B

Writing Short Responses

1a. The variable is not defined.
1b. There is an error in the subtraction.
1c. $79.82 - t = 74.95$
1d. No response, completely incorrect response, or no procedure shown
2. The method is not shown and there is a subtraction error.

Writing Extended Responses

1. It shows all work and answers to both parts of the problem. The response includes an explanation of why this is the complete answer.
2. 1 quarter + 3 nickels equals $0.40, not $0.45.
3. Sample answer: 1 quarter and 2 dimes, 1 quarter and 4 nickels, 3 dimes and 3 nickels; all these add up to $0.45.

Reading for Understanding

1a. the length of the second call
1b. the beginning and ending times of the call
1c. 23 minutes
1d. $1.70
1e. $1.15
1f. $7.80
2a. the pear tree; $\frac{7}{12}$ more bushels
2b. $5\frac{5}{6}$ bushels

Eliminating Answers

1. Since $1\frac{1}{4}$ is less than the original amount, you can immediately eliminate choice B. $4 \times 3 = 12$, so you can eliminate choice A since it would not take into account

the extra $\frac{1}{4}$ cup. 17 is too large since 4×4 is only 16 and $3\frac{1}{4}$ is less than 4. So you can rule out choice D. The correct answer is choice C.
2. You can eliminate choice J; the numbers are almost twice the original numbers. Since 4 is less than half of 9, you can eliminate choice H. The correct answer must be either choice F or choice G.
3. Eliminate choice B; since $\frac{4}{5}$ is nearly equal to 1, 50 is too small. Eliminate choice C; $\frac{4}{5}$ is a fraction less than one, and the answer cannot be larger than the original number. The correct answer is choice A or choice D.

Working Backward

1. C   **2.** G   **3.** D
4. G   **5.** C   **6.** F
7. D   **8.** G   **9.** B

Drawing a Picture

1. $\angle SQR$ (or $\angle RQS$) and $\angle SQP$ (or $\angle PQS$). Since $\overline{SQ}$ and $\overline{PR}$ are perpendicular segments, the angles formed by their intersection are right angles.
2. 51 cm^2; area of the square = $6 \times 6 = 36$ cm^2, area of the triangle = $\frac{1}{2}(6)(5) = 15$ cm^2, and $36 + 15 = 51$.
3. 32°   **4.** 3   **5.** 1
6. a square and a rhombus

Measuring to Solve

1. 75°   **2.** 120°   **3.** 30°   **4.** 140°

Interpreting Data

1. C   **2.** J   **3.** D   **4.** F

Using a Variable

1. Let h = the number of horses. $4h = 84$; $h = 21$; Mr. Drake has 21 horses.
2. Let t = the amount of tax. $17.99 + t = 19.16$; $t = 1.17$; the tax on the DVD is $1.17.
3. Let w = the number of weeks. $18w = 216$; $w = 12$ weeks; Ed bought gas for 12 weeks.
4. Let b = the number of boxes. $3b = 342$; $b = 114$ boxes; Troop 77 sold 114 boxes.
5a. C
5b. $r = 11$ rides

Test-Taking Strategies Course 1 Answers (continued)

Estimating the Answer

1. C; Estimate first. Since the diameter is 1.8 feet, the radius is 0.9 feet. The height is 3.3 feet, which can be rounded to 3 feet. Use 3 for π, 1 for r, and 3 for h in the formula for volume. $V = \pi r^2 h; V \approx 3 \cdot 1 \cdot 3 \approx 9$ ft^3. Choice C is closer to the estimate than the other choices.

2. Estimate using the formula for area of a circle. The diameter of each tablecloth will be $7.8 + 2 = 9.8$ feet, so the radius will be 4.9 feet. Use 5 feet as an estimate. Use 3 for π. $A = \pi r^2; A \approx 3 \cdot 5^2; A \approx 75$ ft^2; $75 \times 10 = 750$ ft^2. She does not have enough material.

3. J

4. C

5. 900 in.^{3}

Name _____ Class _____ Date _____

Test-Taking Strategies Course 2 Answers

Writing Gridded Responses

1. 28.8
2. 12.66
3. 57.66
4. 10.2
5. 2.4 or $\frac{12}{5}$
6. 2
7. 5
8. 48
9. 80
10. 372
11. 150
12. 8
13. 12.06
14. 465
15. 15

Writing Short Responses

1a. Sample answer: 2 points: The equation and the solution are correct. 1 point: The equation is correct but there is an arithmetic error. 0 points: There is no work shown and the solution is incorrect.

1b. Sample answer: $\frac{8.75 - 2.75}{1.5} = 4$ games.

2. Sample answer: Let t = the number of T-shirts.

$$6.99t + 21.99 = 63.93$$
$$6.99t = 41.94$$
$$\frac{6.99t}{6.99} = \frac{41.99}{6.99}$$
$$t = 6$$

Marcus bought 6 T-shirts.

Reading for Understanding

1. 310 feet
2. 140 seconds
3. 1,584 passengers
4. 1.25 miles
5. 4,180 lb
6. Less than 950 kg
7. 14 km or 8.75 mi

Writing Extended Responses

1a. The student added 115.95 to the right side of the equation instead of subtracting. All other work is done correctly.

1b. Sample answer: $42h = \$241.95$; $h = 5.76$ hours

2a. Sample answer: The GCF of 256 and 96 is 32, so Aaron can make 32 bags. The number of purple beads in each bag is $256 \div 32 = 8$; the number of orange beads is $96 \div 21 = 3$.

2b. Sample answer: There should be 16 bags.

Using a Variable

1. $5\frac{1}{4}$ pounds
2. 320 kg
3. 9,741 flashlights
4. $291.84
5. 30 boxes
6. $265.50
7. 120 square feet
8. 18 defective chips
9. 680 pounds
10. 52.5 pounds

Working Backward

1. C
2. G
3. C
4. G
5. D
6. H
7. B
8. G
9. D
10. F
11. D

Drawing a Picture

1. 35°
2. Town J
3. 24°
4. 4 meters
5. −2.2
6. isosceles
7. 16 blocks due west
8. 9
9. 238 square units

Measuring to Solve

1. $r = 3.5$ cm; $C = 21.98$ cm
2. $l = 5$ cm, $w = 2.5$ cm; $P = 15$ cm
3. $s = 5.5$ cm; $A = 30.25$ cm^2

Estimating the Answer

1. A
2. G
3. B
4. H
5. B
6. G
7. C
8. J

Answering the Question Asked

1. A
2. J
3. A
4. G
5. A
6. J
7. C

Interpreting Data

1. C
2. H
3. C
4. H

Eliminating Answers

1a. Percent means per hundred and $\frac{40}{1,000}$ would be less than 400%, or 40%.

1b. D

2a. The denominator needs to be a factor of 30, and 8 is not. Also, since the apples are not all the same color, the probability cannot be 1.

2b. H

3a. The events are independent. You would multiply the probability of each letter selection: 26 times 26 will be greater than 2 and 26.

3b. D

4a. The number of permutations is $_5P_3 = \frac{5!}{2!}$. The answer must be less than 5!, which is 120.

4b. H

Test-Taking Strategies

Course 2

39

Test-Taking Strategies Course 3 Answers

Writing Gridded Responses

1. 55   **2.** 93   **3.** 38   **4.** 5.53   **5.** 32   **6.** 12

Writing Short Responses

1. Sample answer: The first response received two points because it contains a correctly solved equation. The second response received one point because, although it is the correct answer, the student did not set up and solve an equation. The final response received 0 points because it does not have a correct equation and the equation is not solved correctly.

2. Sample answer: Let $x =$ the price of one figurine. $3x + 12.50 = 39.47; 3x = 26.97; x = 8.99;$ Each figurine costs $8.99.

Writing Extended Responses

1.

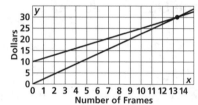

Sample answer: Let $x =$ the number of picture frames sold; Expenses equation: $y = 1.50x + 10.50$; Income equation: $y = 2.25x$. Solution: They must sell 14 picture frames to break even.

2. Sample answer: The student should receive 0 points because, even though the answer is correct, no procedure is shown.

Using a Variable

1. $\frac{9}{12} = \frac{30}{b}; b = 70$ blue marbles

2. $\frac{2.5}{12} = \frac{w}{24}; w = 5$ cm; $\frac{2.5}{12} = \frac{l}{30}; l = 6.25$ cm

3. $\frac{3}{5} = \frac{g}{8.5}; g = 5.1$ ft

4. $\frac{3}{195} = \frac{t}{520}; t = 8$ h

5. $\frac{18}{45} = \frac{28}{l}; l = 70$ m

6. $\frac{1}{8} = \frac{3}{r}; r = 24$ ounces of red; $\frac{1}{8} = \frac{7}{b}; b = 56$ ounces of blue; $\frac{1}{8} = \frac{6}{y}; y = 48$ ounces of yellow

7a. $\frac{2}{9} = \frac{7}{t}; t = 31.5$ h

7b. $\frac{2}{9} = \frac{d}{15}; d = 3.\overline{3}$, or 3 *complete* dresses

Estimating the Answer

1. D   **2.** G   **3.** B   **4.** J   **5.** A
6. G   **7.** C   **8.** G   **9.** C   **10.** F

Reading for Understanding

1. 58.25 in.
2. 11.12 in.
3. Sample answer: The screen is not in the shape of a golden rectangle. The ratio of the longer side to the shorter side is $1.\overline{3}$, which is less than 1.618.

Drawing a Picture

1. 14 units
2. parallelogram $RSUT$ $(6, 1)$ and parallelogram $RSTU$ $(-4, 1)$
3. rhombus
4. no
5. yes
6. 607,904 yd^2
7. 10 blocks
8. $l = 53$ cm, $w = 11$ cm

Eliminating Answers

1. Sample answer: Answer choices A and B can be eliminated because volume should be measured in cubic feet. The answer is either choice C or choice D.
2. D   **3.** F   **4.** C
5. G   **6.** A   **7.** J

Measuring to Solve

1. 32 cm^2 **2.** 6.9 cm^2 **3.** 37.7 cm^2

Answering the Question Asked

1. B   **2.** J   **3.** A   **4.** H
5. A   **6.** F   **7.** A   **8.** H

Interpreting Data

1. D   **2.** F   **3.** C
4. H   **5.** C   **6.** H

Working Backward

1. B   **2.** G   **3.** A   **4.** H
5. B   **6.** J   **7.** C   **8.** G
9. A   **10.** G